BREAK THROUGH

In the same series: *Breakthrough: A Bible Study Tool for Basic Christian Growth*

Breakthrough: A Bible Study Tool for Dynamic Christian Living

BREAK THROUGH

A Bible Study Tool For Basic Christian Assurances

To grow effectively as a Christian, a person must understand God's assurances and apply God's promises.

By Kent M. Fishel and Joel D. DeSelm

First in a series of daily Bible studies on the fundamentals of the Christian life.

Lamplighter Books
Grand Rapids, Michigan
Zondervan Publishing House

First Printing - May, 1980
Second Printing (Revised and Enlarged) - July, 1981
Third Printing (Revised and Enlarged) - November, 1982

Lamplighter Books are published by Zondervan
Publishing House, 1415 Lake Drive, S.E.,
Grand Rapids, Michigan 49506

Cover illustration and cartoons
by Reed Sprunger

Printed in the United States of America

84 85 86 87 88 89 90 / 10 9 8 7 6 5 4 3 2

INTRODUCTION

BREAKTHROUGH was written for young Christians and for those who perhaps are not sure where they stand in their relationship with Jesus Christ. This devotional will serve as an excellent tool to review the basics of the Christian life and the assurances that God gives to each member of His family.

Many people make confessions of faith to Jesus Christ and never quite understand exactly what is expected of them. This booklet will reveal to the readers how they can be totally assured of God's promises in the Bible and know exactly what their responsibilities are to God in light of these Biblical truths.

Frequently, a new convert is given several scripture verses and told, "Here, these are assurances for new Christians. Memorize them and you'll make it." Too often no one teaches new believers how to use, apply or respond to these assurances from God's Word. As a result, many new Christians become frustrated, disillusioned, and even fall away from the faith because of improper follow-through and discipleship training. Sensing this void, the authors set out to write a series of devotional books dealing with the needs of the new believer.

The BREAKTHROUGH series works best in a small group study or in a one-to-one situation. However, it can also be a challenging study when used on an individual basis. For maximum effectiveness, the following format is suggested: Read the verse at the top of the page. Then read through the devotional, considering how the scripture passage relates to the thoughts shared. Fill in the blanks and answer the questions honestly and openly. Complete the application project as listed. By applying this project, you will internalize and personalize the truths from God's Word you have studied. Finally, be sure to check out **"Appendix A"** to find **other related scriptures** for your quiet time.

May Christ richly bless you as you daily walk in the strength and power of His Word!

In Jesus' Love,
Kent and Joel

"Therefore, if anyone is in Christ, he is a new creation; the old has gone, the new has come!" II Cor. 5:17 (NIV)

Day 1 – YOU ARE LOVED

Have you ever wished you could leave home and start all over again in a city where no one knew anything about you? You probably thought, "by moving away, I'll be able to be different; I'll change." Chances are even if you would have gone to a new location, your problems would still be with you! Why?

Because lasting changes come from the inside - out.

God tells you this kind of a "inner" change can take place without running away from your environment, problems, or your fears.

God loves you! He loves you so much that He sent His only Son Jesus Christ to earth to die on the cross for your sins. On the third day, God raised Jesus from the dead. Today, Jesus is with God in heaven. Jesus, even though He had never sinned, chose to die on the cross for your sins and rose from the grave conquering death. YOU can be changed and have new life in Christ. To receive Christ you must admit you are a sinner, acknowledge Christ's sacrifice for your sins, and personally accept what Christ the Son of God did for you by inviting Him to come into your heart and life. At that moment when you receive Christ by a specific act of your will, the Holy Spirit enters your being. Jesus comes into your life. His life in you gives you the power to live a new kind of life. You now are changed from the inside - out. You are a Christian, "a new creation in Christ!"

1. Write in your own words what II Cor. 5:17 means. ____________________

____

____

2. According to II Cor. 5:17 if __________ is in Christ that person is a new creation.

3. What does it mean to be a new creation in Christ? (See the last part of IICor. 5:17) ____________________

____

____

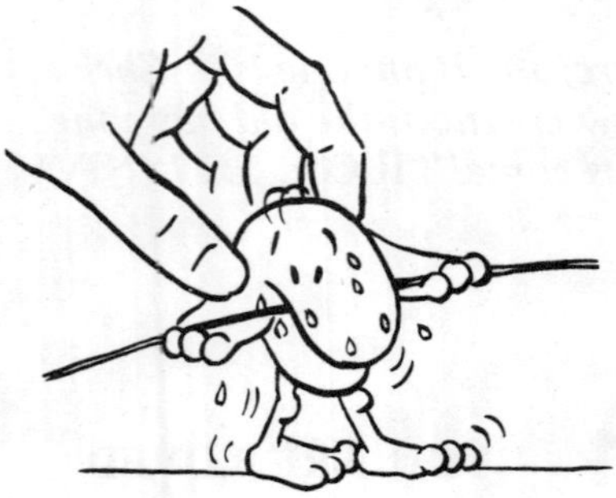

"Yet to all who received Him, to those who believed in His name, He gave the right to become children of God." John 1:12 (NIV)

Day 2 – WALK WHAT YOU TALK!

You receive Christ into your life when you by personal invitation ask Him to come in and forgive you of your sins; you then determine each day to be obedient to His word and the leading of His Holy Spirit. Perhaps you may be thinking, "How do I know if I **really** asked Jesus to come in? What does believing in Jesus mean?"

The story is told of a man who one day pushed a wheelbarrow across Niagara Falls on a tightrope. As the man was coming across the rope balancing himself, a spectator turned to his friend and loudly said, "Let's leave. We've seen this act before; I believe that man could walk across Niagara Falls a hundred times!"

As this individual continued the discussion with his friend, the aerial performer stepped safely onto solid ground amidst much applause. He overheard the conversation between the two men and immediately confronted the man who wanted to leave.

"Do you really believe I could do this performance 100 times successfully?" he asked. The man, somewhat taken off guard, quickly responded, "Well, yes, I do!" The performer looked straight into the man's eyes and said, "Good. **You** hop in the wheelbarrow, and I will take you across."

After the man quickly refused, the tightrope walker asked, "You said you believe that I can do it. Why won't you go with me?"

The man, as he prepared to leave, shouted, "I believe you can, but there's no way I'M getting into that wheelbarrow!"

Friend, believing in Jesus Christ is more than just spitting out the words. You need to "get into the wheelbarrow." Being a Christian is more than just talking about Jesus. It is coming to the place where you die to self and then desire Jesus to be in control of each area of your life.

Picture yourself signing your name to a blank contract for life and saying, "Jesus, daily I will do what You want me to. I will be obedient to your Word. I yield my rights, my attitudes, and my actions to you. Jesus, I can trust You not only to forgive me of my sins, but also I can trust You to help me become the person God wants me to be."

Have you gotten "into the wheelbarrow?" YES NO

Have you signed this contract with Jesus? YES NO

"Here I am! I stand at the door and knock. If anyone hears my voice and opens the door, I will go in and eat with him and he with Me."
Rev. 3:20 (NIV)

Day 3 – KNOCK KNOCK - WHO'S THERE?

If you have not yet invited Jesus Christ to come into your life, you can do it right now.

Read Revelation 3:20. Write in your own words what this verse is saying:

____

____

Jesus is knocking on the door of your life. When someone knocks at a door, that person is trying to get the attention of someone on the inside. Jesus wants to get your attention.

How has Jesus been trying to speak to you? ______________________

____

____

When the person on the inside hears someone knocking outside, that person has three choices: First, (1) he/she can ignore the knocking, Secondly, (2) he/she can tell the person to go away, or Thirdly, (3) this individual can choose to open the door and invite whoever is on the outside to come in.

Jesus Christ, the Son of God, is knocking at your heart's door, the will of your life. Circle the choice of the number which describes how you wish to respond to Jesus: 1, 2, 3.
Explain: ______________________________________

____

If by definite act of your will you invite Him to come into your life, He will enter and take control. This invitation to accept Jesus is admitting you have sin in your life and need His forgiveness and cleansing. You must come to the place where you no longer desire to run your own life. You acknowledge that Jesus provided the only way for forgiveness of sins. Jesus took your sins and offers you His righteousness.

Reread Rev. 3:20. Before Jesus comes into my life I must:

1) ______________________________

2) ______________________________

Then God will do His part:

1) ______________________________

2) ______________________________

If you have not yet invited Jesus Christ to come into your life, do it right now. Pray a prayer similar to this:

Dear God,

I admit that I am a sinner. I know that Jesus Christ died on the cross for my sins; I now want to receive Him into my heart and life. Forgive me, Jesus, for my sins. Lord, I give You the right to do in my life whatever You want to do. Help me, dear God, one day at a time to walk in obedience to Your Word. Jesus, thank you for coming into my heart, forgiving my sins, and giving to me eternal life.

In Jesus' Name, AMEN

I prayed the above prayer on ______________________
DATE

____
SIGNATURE

Some of you who read this are not sure whether or not you have received Jesus into your life. You may pray a prayer something like this:

Lord Jesus,

I am not sure if I am really a Christian. Jesus, if I have not received you before, right now I invite you to come into my life. Forgive me of my sins and make me a part of Your family.

Thank you for dying for my sins and forgiving me. I know you have heard my prayer and I now have eternal life!

In Jesus' Name, AMEN

If I had never received Jesus Christ before, I definitely did on

____
DATE

____
SIGNATURE

According to Titus 3:5-8, I know my salvation is not because of ______________________ but because of God's ______________________.

"So then, just as you received Christ Jesus as Lord, continue to live in Him, rooted and built up in Him."
Colossians 2:6,7 (NIV)

Day 4 – ON YOUR MARK, GET SET, GROW!

You considered yesterday how God promises in His Word that Christians have eternal life. That promise is a FACT; facts do not change. Regardless of your many doubts, fears, and failures during your Christian life, God STILL says that as a child of God, you will go to heaven.

Yet, with this assurance comes a responsibility on YOUR part as well. Receiving Jesus Christ and eternal life involves more than just a fire insurance policy to keep you out of hell. Jesus wants to not only be your Saviour, but your **Lord** as well.

What does it mean to have Jesus Christ as Lord of your life? This involves doing things His way, as revealed in the Bible, rather than going your own selfish way. Christ as Lord means to surrender to Him your will and desires, giving Him your thoughts, habits, speech, and actions. He wants to control all your decisions concerning your future, your dating relationships, your lifestyle, etc.

Jesus becomes Lord of your life as you daily study the Bible and surrender your will to Him by obeying these truths. The better you know Christ, the more you will be able to trust Him. Through Bible reading, you will be able to replace <u>your</u> way of doing things with God's scriptural guidelines. As Christ's Word controls your thoughts and actions, you will experience more of the abundant life He promises.

Notice in Colossians 2:6,7 you are to be ____________________

and ____________ in Christ. To do this, you must daily grow in your

commitment to Jesus by getting fresh nourishment from His __________.
You WILL be built up (growing) in Christ by:

(circle each correct response)

A. Being obedient to the Word of God.
B. Confessing your sins as soon as the Holy Spirit reveals them to you.
C. Attending a Bible-preaching and teaching church.
D. Spending quality time with Christian friends.
E. Talking and listening to the Lord every day.
F. Subjecting yourself to those in authority over you.
(parents, teachers, youth leader)

If you circled all of the above responses, you're right! They are all important ways to be in the process of maturing in Christ. How about you?

Are you growing in Christ? ______________

"For I am convinced that neither death nor life, neither angels nor demons, neither the present nor the future, nor any powers, neither height nor depth, nor anything else in all creation, will be able to separate us from the love of God that is in Christ Jesus our Lord." Romans 8:38,39 (NIV)

Day 5 – YOU ARE "SPECIAL!"

Do you ever feel unloved? Do you feel unlovely? As a believer in Christ, do you still seem to fail again and again? It is easy to feel unimportant and unloveable. Your feelings constantly change, and your failures can continue to remind you of how unworthy you are, sometimes causing you to even question if God loves you any more. HOWEVER . . . GOD'S ATTITUDE TOWARD **YOU** DOES NOT CHANGE! GOD LOVES **YOU** REGARDLESS OF HOW LOUSY **YOU** FEEL OR HOW OFTEN **YOU** FAIL!

According to Romans 8:38,39 what can separate us from the love of God?__________. One cannot earn or deserve God's love - it is by grace that He loves each of us. Look up Ephesians 2:8,9. Salvation is God's gift to me when I place my __________ in Jesus. According to this verse a person is not saved by __________. "Grace" is Christ loving you when you are undeserving and unlovely. And He still loves you the same, no matter what you do, think, or feel.

YOU are valuable. **YOU** are worthwhile. **YOU** are special to God. How do you know? Would He have given His Son up to die for your sins if **you** weren't extremely important to Him? God loved you enough to send His Son to die for you while YOU were rebellious, sinful, unworthy, and undeserving. "But God demonstrates His own love for us in this: While we were still sinners, Christ died for us." (Romans 5:8) What is amazing about God's love? ____

____

What a wonderful Father our God is! Your attitude, in response to God's love for you should be one of gratitude, praise, and worship. Your actions, then, should reflect your love for Him.

Go back and re-read this devotional, substituting your first name for each bold "you."

"If you love me, you will obey what I command." John 14:15 (NIV)

Day 6 – YOU HAVE A RESPONSIBILITY!

Yesterday, you looked at the assurance of God's love, regardless of your feelings, your faults, and your failures. Does that mean, then, that you can talk, think, and act however you desire because God will still love you anyway? Not really. YOU HAVE A RESPONSIBILITY IN THE WAY YOU RESPOND TO GOD'S LOVE.

His love should motivate and empower you to grow and become like Christ by your obeying and applying the scriptures. Because of His great love for you, you have the freedom to live more like Jesus, without the threat of rejection when you stumble or fall.

You need to guard, however, against the attitude of just sitting back and living like you please, being satisfied with your faults and not attempting to change them. God didn't rescue you from your old ways of doing things just to let you fall back into them; His eternal love isn't an excuse or license for you to live as you please. Instead, His love gives you the freedom and the power to enable you to become more like Jesus Christ each day.

How are **you** responding to the love of God? God's love is not intended to make you feel rejected, shameful, or condemned. Neither is His love for you a cop-out allowing you to live any way you want. Instead, be assured that His love is unchanging, eternal, and powerful, helping you to become more Christ-like.

1. According to John 14:15 what is a true indication of my love for God?

____

2. Look up these commands and then list your responsibilities:

   A. II Timothy 2:15 - My responsibility is to ______________

   B. Ephesians 6:1,2 - My responsibility is to ______________

   C. Philippians 2:3,4 - My responsibility is to ______________

   D. II Timothy 2:22 - My responsibility is to ______________

   E. Joshua 1:8 - My responsibility is to ______________

   F. Proverbs 28:13 - My responsibility is to ______________

   G. I Thessalonians 5:18 - My responsibility is to ______________

   H. I Thessalonians 5:17 - My responsibility is to ______________

   I. Mark 5:19 - My responsibility is to ______________

"Your Word is a lamp to my feet and a light to my path."
Psalm 119:105 (NIV)

Day 7 – FEELINGS CAN BE MISLEADING

Just like the weather, your feelings are very unpredictable. As a Christian, God wants you to be controlled by His Holy Spirit and His Word, not by your feelings. The dictionary states that feelings are "emotions." Describe three influences that dictate how you feel during the day:

1. ________________ 2. ________________ 3. ________________

Romans 3:22 explains that you become a Christian by placing your ________ in Jesus Christ. Faith is described in Hebrews 11:1, as: ________
__________________________ and __________________________

Notice in Hebrews 13:8 that ____________________ is the same
____________________, ____________________, AND ______________ .

Look up Matthew 24:35. Jesus says, "My ______________ shall not pass away."

Unlike your feelings, Jesus Christ and His Word **do not** change. Jesus Christ, the Living Word, and the Bible, the inspired Word of God, are true. If you choose to "accept" and "obey" the Word of God, you will always be living according to His purposes for your life.

To understand this difference between faith and feelings, look at the illustration below:

A train engine powered by coal only needs the coal car to run. It can run with or without the boxcars or caboose. Likewise, while feelings and circumstances play a significant part in your life, your assurance of salvation and your continuing relationship with God through Jesus Christ is <u>not</u> based upon feelings or circumstances. "Feelings" are not necessary for you to know you are a Christian.

(continued on next page)

Unless you daily place your faith in the fact of Jesus Christ and the Word of God, you will be pulled downward spiritually. "Keep on keeping on" with Jesus Christ by daily walking in obedience to the Word of God!

PRAYER: Thank you, Jesus, that even though my feelings and circumstances change, I know that I am a Christian because I have placed my faith and trust in the unchangeable fact that you died for my sins and provided eternal life for me. I want to daily walk in obedience to the truth of Your Word. Help me, Jesus, to walk by faith in the promises found in the Bible and not allow my feelings and circumstances to control me. In Your Name, Jesus, Amen.

"MY HOPE IS BUILT ON NOTHING LESS
THAN JESUS' BLOOD AND RIGHTEOUSNESS;
I DARE NOT TRUST THE SWEETEST FRAME
BUT WHOLLY LEAN ON JESUS' NAME;
ON CHRIST THE SOLID ROCK; I STAND,
ALL OTHER GROUND IS SINKING SAND."

FOR FURTHER READING: *Basic Christianity*
by John Stott, Inter-Varsity Press

Know Why You Believe
by Paul Little, Inter-Varsity Press

"And this is the testimony: God has given us eternal life, and this life is in His Son. He who has the Son has life; he who does not have the Son of God does not have life." I John 5:11-12 (NIV)

Day 8 – LET'S GET PERSONAL!

Circle each letter which is followed by the statements that best complete this sentence:

"One becomes a child of God by . . . "

A. attending church regularly.
B. inviting Jesus Christ into your life.
C. being born into a Christian family.
D. believing and receiving Jesus as Savior and Lord.
E. faith in Christ Jesus.
F. trying your best to do good things.
G. knowing all the facts about Jesus' life and His work on earth.

The correct answers are: b. - see Revelation 3:20 d. - see John 1:12 e. - see Ephesians 2:8,9

When did you become a Christian? ______________
DATE

Briefly explain how this happened: ______________________________
____
____
____
____

Which verse of scripture means the most to you in your salvation experience?

______________ (suggestions: John 3:16, Acts 16:31, John 1:12, etc.)

"I write these things to you who believe in the name of the Son of God so that you may know that you have eternal life."
I John 5:13 (NIV)

Day 9 – ASSURANCE THROUGH GOD'S WORD!

Going to church, living by the Golden Rule, or obeying the Ten Commandments does not make you a Christian! The Bible says that you are a Christian if you admit to God that you are a sinner (have fallen short of God's standard of holiness in your life), believe that Jesus Christ died for your sins, and personally ask Christ to come into your life to make you into the type of person He wants you to be. See Revelation 3:20.

You can KNOW 100%, beyond the shadow of a doubt, that you will go to heaven. This is a **fact.** God promises eternal life to those who have a new life in Christ Jesus (see I John 5:11-13). Yet, many Christians still wonder, wish, or only hope they will go to heaven - the Bible says that you can KNOW! If Christ is in your life, you have ________________________.

How do you know this? ____

If you have met God's requirement of admitting your sin, believing Christ died for your sin, and personally inviting Him into your life to control you and make you new, you can be TOTALLY assured and confident that you will go to heaven. God has promised heaven to you and WANTS you to be sure.

Does God lie? Is the Bible lying to you when it says in I John 5:13 that you have eternal life? Of course not! Even though your feelings change, the fact of your salvation does not change. You may not "feel" like a Christian at times - THIS DOES NOT MEAN SUDDENLY YOU ARE NO LONGER A CHRISTIAN. Put your trust and faith in the FACT and TRUTH of God and His Word - not in your changeable feelings!

According to I John 5:13, the Bible was written so ________________________
YOUR NAME

(CIRCLE THE ONE CORRECT ANSWER)
may (hope, guess, feel, think, know, wish) that ________________________
YOUR NAME

(CIRCLE THE ONE CORRECT ANSWER)
(qualifies for church membership, can be religious, has eternal life).

Remember, this is a promise to you from ______________.

"Those who live according to the sinful nature have their minds set on what that nature desires; but those who live in accordance with the Spirit have their minds set on what the Spirit desires."
Romans 8:5 (NIV)

Day 10 – ASSURANCE THROUGH A CHANGED LIFE!

Not only can you have assurance of salvation in Christ through His Word (I John 5:11-15) (Rev. 3:20) and (John 1:12) but also by seeing a change in your attitudes and desires.

Dig into the Word of God today and discover 9 evidences that demonstrate Christ is in your heart and life. You will not have matured in all of these areas; make it your desire and purpose to allow the Holy Spirit freedom to help you as a Christian develop these qualities each day:

1. See John 3:30 - I have a desire to have God ___________ in my life.
2. See I Peter 2:2 - I have a desire to read _________________.
3. See II Corinthians 5:17 - I have a new _______________ in Christ.
4. See I John 2:15, 16 - I no longer love the things of this _________.
5. See Psalm 119:9-11 - I desire not to _______________________.
6. See II Timothy 3:12 - I expect __________________ as a Christian.
7. See I John 4:7, 8 - I have a growing __________ for other Christians.
8. See I Peter 3:15 - I need to _____________ to others about my new life in Christ.
9. See James 4:7 - I now have a desire to resist __________________.

"For you did not receive a spirit that makes you a slave again to fear, but you received the Spirit of sonship. And by him we cry, "Abba, Father." The Spirit himself testifies with our spirit that we are God's children." Romans 8:15,16 (NIV)

Day 11 – ASSURANCE THROUGH THE HOLY SPIRIT!

The final way you know Jesus is in your life is through the Holy Spirit confirming this new birth experience with the Spirit of Christ within you.

When you give Christ the right to do in your life whatever He wants to do, you allow Him to be Lord. This is a daily "process" of trusting Him and obeying the Holy Spirit as He leads you into God's truth.

Read Galatians 5:22-24. As a Spirit-controlled Christian your life will produce these characteristics of the friut of the Spirit:

__________, __________, __________, __________, __________,

__________, __________, __________, and __________.

Name one fruit of the Spirit which is evident in your life. __________
Explain specifically the ways in which this fruit is being demonstrated in

your everyday living: ______________________________

____

____

Read Galatians 5:14 - 21. These characteristics of your old nature are now dead in Christ.

You must moment by moment choose to demonstrate the qualities of Jesus Christ and not the characteristics of your old fleshly nature.

You choose to obey the Word of God each day one step at a time.

Philippians 4:13 says, "I can do__________things through Christ who strengthens, and enables me."

Today, God, you want me to take the characteristic of (name one)

__________and demonstrate this area of the Fruit of the Spirit to (name

person) __________ by doing this (specific act) ______________________________

____

______________________________.

"When they saw the courage of Peter and John and realized that they were unschooled; ordinary men, they were astonished and they took note that these men had been with Jesus." Acts 4:13 (NIV)

Day 12 – "TYING UP LOOSE ENDS!"

You have studied three ways which assure you of eternal life.

1. The Word of God assures it.
2. A changed life demonstrates it.
3. The Holy Spirit confirms it.

According to Acts 4:13, how did the people explain Peter and John's changed lives?______________________________

How has your life changed since you have become a Christian?

1) ______________________________

2) ______________________________

3) ______________________________

After by faith I received Christ into my life, I know He came in because:

(CIRCLE THE ONE CORRECT ANSWER)

A. I feel differently than I did before.
B. I shed tears.
C. I did what another person told me to do.
D. I know this is what the Bible said Jesus would do for me.

Do you know you have eternal life?__________

How do you know? ______________________________

____

What verse in the Bible best assures YOU of eternal life; Copy it here:

____

"God said it in His Word
I believe it in my heart
That settles it forever!"

"For the wages of sin is death, but the gift of God is eternal life in Christ Jesus our Lord." Romans 6:23 (NIV)

Day 13 – "UNWRAP GOD'S GIFT!"

In the scripture verse you just read, you discovered God has a ________ for you. When you by faith ask Jesus Christ into your life, you receive a beautiful "package plan."

Unwrap "this gift from God" by looking up the following verses and claiming the promises God has for you:

1. My ________ were forgiven by ________. (See I John 1:9 and Colossians 1:13,14)

2. ________ came to live in my life. (See Galatians 2:20) From this verse

   where is Jesus now living? ____________________

3. I have become a ____________ of God. (See John 1:12,13)

4. I have been promised an ___________ life in Christ. (See John 10:10)

5. I have the promise of ______________________________. (See John 3:16)

6. I have an ___________ as God's son or daughter. (See Romans 8:16,17)

   As a heir, in God's family, one gift God has given to me is ____________.

7. I have new ________________ through the Holy Spirit. (See John 16:13)

8. I have new ________________. (See Philippians 4:13)

9. I have new ________________. (See John 14:27)

10. I am now an ________________ for Christ. (See II Cor. 5:20)

Having claimed the above assurances, now go back and thank God specifically for each one of these promises.

"I will cleanse them from all the sin they have committed against Me and will forgive all their sin of rebellion against Me." Jeremiah 33:8 (NIV)

Day 14 – CONFESSION COMES FIRST

If a son is arrested for running a red light and his father pays the fine, the penalty has been paid as far as the courts are concerned. Yet, the father, who is displeased with his son for breaking the law, must still talk some things over with him to restore their fellowship with one another. The boy is still the father's son - their **relationship** is permanent. However, there has been a block in the **fellowship** between the father and the son!

As a Christian, your relationship with God being your Father and your being His son is permanent. Yet, when you sin, your fellowship and communion with God has been broken and must be healed. As with the boy running the red light, you must admit that wrong and ask your Father's forgiveness.

This is done by confessing your sin to God. "Confess" means to "agree with" or to "call the same thing." You must "agree with" God that what you did was wrong and "call it the same thing" as He calls it.

Confessing your sins and claiming God's forgiveness was part of your **becoming** a Christian and will continue to be a way of **remaining** in close fellowship with Him. You need to confess the action or attitude immediately, being honest with God. You must agree with God that it is sin, claiming forgiveness and thanking Him for His cleansing.

Is there sin in your life right now that you need to confess to God?_____

Remember, sin is rebellion against God. From Jeremiah 33:8, how much of your sin will God forgive?___________ You can confess your sin to God any time and anywhere. Agree with God that you have sinned and ask Him to forgive you.

After you receive Christ into your life, can you still sin?____________
See I John 1:8, 10.

When you do sin, after you become a Christian, will God forgive you?

___________(See I John 1:9 - remember, John's letter was written to Christians!)

"If we confess our sins, He is faithful and just and will forgive us our sins and purify us from all unrighteousness."
I John 1:9 (NIV)

Day 15 – FORGIVENESS FOLLOWS NEXT

After you have confessed your sin, notice I John 1:9 states that God

is ____________ and ____________ to forgive you of your ____________

and purify you from all ____.

God's forgiveness takes place in heaven. Imagine a chalk board with writing on it. Someone takes an eraser and erases all of the writing. Nothing is left on the chalk board; the writing is completely gone.

As a Christian, through the righteousness of Jesus Christ who died for your sins, God removes the penalty of these sins as you confess them to Him. Look up Hebrews 10:17,18. From this verse, what is God's attitude toward

your "confessed" sins? ____

Not only does God forgive your sins, according to I John 1:9, He

____________ you. This means you are made clean through Christ's sacrifice for your sins on the cross. What sin does God want you to confess to Him right now? Confess it and claim God's glorious forgiveness and cleansing.

God, I confess to you ____.

What **specific** steps do you need to take to overcome this sinful habit or desire in your life?

1) ____

2) ____

3) ____

"But if we walk in the light, as He is in the light, we have fellowship with one another, and the blood of Jesus, His Son, purifies us from every sin."
I John 1:7 (NIV)

Day 16 – "SPIRITUAL BREATHING"

How often should you confess your sins? Well, how often should you take a shower? Obviously, as often as necessary to stay clean!

Try this little exercise. Exhale . . . then deeply inhale! Breathe in this exaggerated way 5 times. Now, keep on breathing normally!

Think of exhaling as confessing your sins to God and inhaling as taking in God's forgiveness and cleansing.

Just like you must continue to physically breathe to stay alive physically, you must continue to "spiritually breathe" to stay alive spiritually!

Are you practicing spiritual breathing every day? ____________________

If you aren't, you aren't spiritually clean!

When you confess your sins, God restores your fellowship to Himself. Notice in the verse above He promises to those who "walk in the light" (walking in fellowship with God) two things - Name them:

1) ____

2) ____

Prayer:

Dear God, give me lungs for Jesus. As soon as the Holy Spirit reveals I have sinned, help me to immediately confess my sin that I may instantly be forgiven and restored to a right fellowship with you. In Jesus Name, Amen.

Sin brings enmity; **Christ brings Peace**
Sin creates a gulf between man and God; **Christ bridges the gap**
Sin breaks fellowship; **Christ restores it**

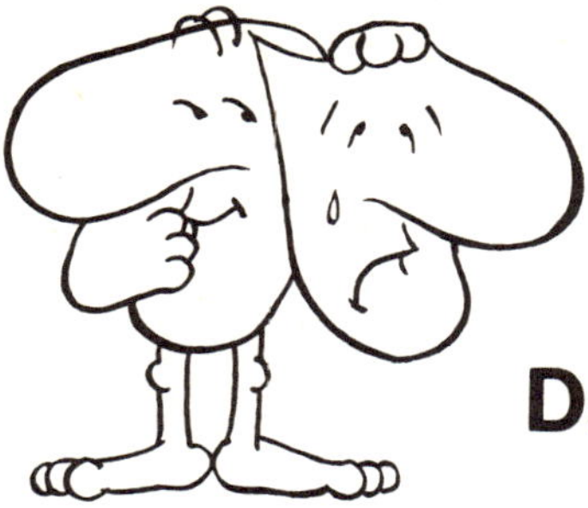

"There is a way that seems right to man but in the end it leads to death."
Proverbs 16:25 (NIV)

Day 17 – COUNTERFEIT CONFESSION

Today, you need to recognize the counterfeit actions which are most often used when you do not practice the truth of I John 1:9 in your daily living.

Many people choose to do things their **own** way instead of doing what **God** tells them to do. This is often done through rationalization (making up reasons to justify what you are doing even though you know these reasons are not legitimate.)

Some forms of rationalizing sin in your life are:

1. Ignore it - trying to forget about it - "I just won't think about it"
2. Excuse it - "The reason I . . . "
3. Minimize it - "It really wasn't so bad . . ." - "It's not that big of a deal!"
4. Compare it - "Lots of people do it" - "Everyone else is doing it"
5. Blame it on someone else - "But (Jon) told me to" - "Whenever I get near (Jon), he makes me . . ."
6. Compensate for it - "I go to church" - "I give money for the offering"
7. Postpone it - "Next Sunday I'll confess it . . ."

Go back and circle the two forms of rationalization you use most often when you don't practice God's way of dealing with sin, I John 1:9.

If you choose to ignore God's way of dealing with sin, and go your own way, God's Word in Proverbs 16:25 promises you will have spiritual

______________________________.

"He who conceals his sins does not prosper, but whoever confesses and renounces them finds mercy."
Proverbs 28:13 (NIV)

Day 18 – THE CONSEQUENCES OF CONCEALMENT

Now that you have seen man's way of dealing with sin, you need to realize its consequences.

As you have seen in I John 1:9, if you don't ______________ your sins, then your sins are not ______________ nor are you ______________.

Therefore, you are accountable for these sins.

Maybe you are thinking, "Wow, what if I overlooked a sin; what will happen to me then?" As a Christian, God's Holy Spirit, Who resides in you, will reveal to you each sin you have committed.

Again, you must understand as a Christian if you don't deal with sin in your life, you won't receive God's forgiveness and blessings.

Picture an electric train which has several cars behind it. As the train goes around a curve, one of the cars falls off with its wheels touching the track. This causes a short circuit. The train is still a train, but it can't function properly without the necessary flow of electrical power.

In the same way, sin forms a barrier in your relationship to God. As a believer in Christ, you are no longer functioning the way God wants you to when you allow sin to continue in your life!

Proverbs 28:13 says if you ______________ your sins, you will not ______________________.

As a Christian, if you confess your sins, you will continue to have God's __________________.

"As far as the east is from the west, so far has He removed our transgressions from us." Psalm 103:12 (NIV)

Day 19 – DANGER ZONES

As a Christian, God will forgive your sins if you confess them to Him. Yet, there are two dangerous attitudes you might fall into concerning confession and forgiveness.

The first is that you may not be able to accept the fact that your sins are truly forgiven. You might choose to wallow in shame and think that you must "feel" guilty and miserable for what you have done before God will really forgive you. There should be a certain sorrow and remorse for your sins, but you cannot "pay" for your sin by feeling rotten and guilty - Jesus has paid the full penalty for sin. **Confess** your sin to God through Jesus and **accept** His cleansing.

Even though God forgets the sin and restores your fellowship with Himself, you could still feel worthless, despised, and unacceptable for having goofed up again - even after having confessed and having been forgiven of your sin. God doesn't want you to feel dejected and miserable. One of the privileges of being a Christian is that you can be forgiven and freed from your guilt and shame. Believe God loves you and accepts you!

The second extreme you can take as a Christian is to use God's forgiveness as a license and excuse to sin. Besides confessing your sin, God wants you to "repent" of your sin; He wants you to turn away and replace your old thoughts and actions with His thoughts and behavior patterns as revealed in the Bible. You cannot be a growing Christian and play on the love and patience of God by sinning as much as you want. There must be a responsibility on your part to pray and work in that area of your life, with Christ's help, so that you can become the person that He wants you to be. Determine to go in God's direction right now!

In your own words, what does Psalm 103:12 mean? _______________

____

To stay healthy as a Christian you must:

A - Admit you are a sinner, in need of DAILY forgiveness and cleansing that only Christ can provide.

B - Believe that Christ's dying on the cross paid the ENTIRE debt for you, enabling God to forgive your sins.

C - Claim God's forgiveness, cleansing, and restored fellowship.

D - Determine in the strength of Christ to resist the temptation to sin.

"No temptation has seized you except what is common to man. And God is faithful; He will not let you be tempted beyond what you can bear. But when you are tempted, He will also provide a way out so that you can stand up under it."
I Corinthians 10:13 (NIV)

20 – WHAT IS TEMPTATION?

Many people are bewildered when they discover that they still face temptations after having received Christ into their lives! However, just as exercise makes an athlete strong, temptation can make a Christian strong too. Temptation is the desire to do something God has said not to do. Temptation is not sin - giving in to the temptation is sin. Temptation will not hurt you unless you yield to it - in fact, temptation will strengthen your faith and help you to grow.

Temptation comes from three sources. Identify them from the verses below:

I John 2:15, 16 - ______________________

James 1:13, 14 - ______________________

Matthew 4:3 - ______________________

The world refers to the overall attitude of society, the general thinking of unbelievers, and the negative influence of peer pressure. The flesh pertains to the pride and selfishness that comes from the desires of your mind and body. The devil relates to Satan's influences in trying to convince you that God's standards are wrong and that you should believe him, rather than Christ.

To be victorious over temptation you **must** be in close fellowship with God, you must pray and ask Him for help at the time of need, and you must be saturated with God's Word in order to overcome the temptation. God promises to help - but you must turn to Him, and then **act** in obedience to His Word!

According to I Corinthians 10:13, circle the correct response in each pair below:

A. Your temptations are more difficult than those of others.
B. The temptation you face has been and is being faced by other people.

A. God allows you to be tempted in ways you can't handle to put you down.
B. God will never allow you to face a temptation or trial greater than that which you can endure in His Strength.

(continued on next page)

A. God is sometimes too busy and chooses to ignore you when you need Him.
B. God will always help you if you look to Him for your strength.

A. God wants you to be defeated so He lets your problems conquer you.
B. God provides ways to overcome temptation if you are obedient to His Word.

A. You will never be tempted if you are walking close to God.
B. Nobody is immune to temptation. Jesus wasn't; you won't be either.

(ANSWERS: IN EACH CASE "B" IS THE CORRECT ANSWER)

Wrong is wrong even if everybody is doing it.

Right is right even if no one is doing it.

FOR FURTHER READING: *Freedom from Guilt*
by Bruce Narramore and Bill Counts
Harvest House Publishers

The New You
by Harold Myra, Zondervan

"Be self-controlled and alert. Your enemy the devil prowls around like a roaring lion looking for someone to devour." I Peter 5:8 (NIV)

Day 21 – BE ON THE LOOKOUT!

Even though God promises you that **He** will help you in time of temptation, **you** have a responsibility as well. You can't expect God to help you overcome temptation unless you are obedient to His Word.

First, in today's verse you learn to EXPECT temptation. Temptation is normal and common. When you expect it, you will not be surprised when temptation comes, and you will be better prepared to handle it. Notice in I Peter 5:8, the devil is compared to a ____________________. The animals that survive are those animals who anticipate and expect the enemy who is seeking to destroy them.

Peter is telling you to be alert and under self-control so that you will not give in to your enemy, Satan. Circle the words that describe the attitude you should have about "temptation" according to I Peter 5:8. (be watchful, anticipate temptation, ignore temptation, be attentive, disregard temptation, be on your toes). Name the temptation that you must be alert for today:

____

Secondly, you must RECOGNIZE temptation - not only when it comes from wrong desires, but also when the temptation entices you to overindulge in right desires. Obviously, you must not only expect temptation; you must also be able to recognize it. I Peter 5:8 states the lion is out to ______________. He is not out to "nip your heels" or scratch you up a bit. The devil is out to ruin you, and you must recognize temptation for what it is - a means to defeat you in your Christian walk and wipe out your relationship with Christ.

"Flee the evil desires of youth . . ."
II Timothy 2:22 (NIV)

Day 22 – WATCH YOUR STEP!

Not only are you to expect and recognize temptation, but the Bible also instructs you to FLEE temptation. What are some words or phrases that are suggested by the verb "flee?" ______________________

To flee does NOT mean you are to rationalize, toy with, walk away, or back off from temptation. Rather, "flee" means to run, to escape to deliberately move in the opposite direction. If you **immediately** turn from the temptation and mentally/physically travel in a different direction, then temptation cannot destroy you or lead you into sin.

Along with fleeing temptation, you are to AVOID temptation as well. In I Thessalonians 5:22, God tells you to "avoid every kind of __________ __________." Another translation reads "avoid the very appearance of evil." Eve would not have been tempted by the fruit if she had not been standing near the forbidden tree. Avoid getting yourself into a potentially dangerous situation. You know your weaknesses and where you easily fall. Don't purposely ask for trouble!

Romans 13:14 says ". . . do not think about how to gratify the desires of the sinful nature." In your own words, write out what Romans 13:14 is saying: ____

______________________. You are more susceptible to temptation when you are physically and spiritually run-down. Be aware of this. At what time do **you** find yourself tempted the most? ______________

____.

"Because He Himself suffered when He was tempted, He is able to help those who are being tempted." Hebrews 2:18 (NIV)

Day 23 – HELP IS AVAILABLE!

When you are tempted, you can have victory over the temptation through the enabling power of Jesus. You are no match for the devil; but in the strength of Christ, the devil is no match for you! According to Hebrews 2:18, what is Jesus able to do? ______________________
In what form will this help come? Circle the two correct phrases - (the Lord will: mystically change you into a super-human, enable you to turn from the temptation, "zap" you with spirituality, encourage you and fill your mind with His thoughts as you dwell on His Word.)

This help Jesus provides is not just available after the temptation or after you sin, but while you are "being tempted." Look up Hebrews 4:15. From this verse, why is Jesus able to understand the temptations you are going through and, therefore, give you just the help and victory you need?

____

Jesus knows what you are going through. He went through it. Every temptation you face, Jesus has already faced. He not only has **been** there, He has been **victorious**! You need only "approach the throne of grace with confidence to find grace to help you in your time of need." (Hebrews 4:16)

How should you go to Christ when you need help to overcome temptation? Check out these verses and match the letter of the verse to your responsibility in drawing upon Christ's power when you face temptation:

A. Isaiah 59:1,2	______	Pray for God's strength and deliverance.
B. Matt. 6:9,13	______	Yield your will and rights to God; thus you withstand Satan's attacks.
C. Psalm 119:9,11	______	Make sure you have confessed known sin to God.
D. James 4:7	______	Remember that temptations, when resisted, help you to become stronger in your Christian life.
E. James 1:2,3	______	Fill your mind with God's Word and obey these truths.

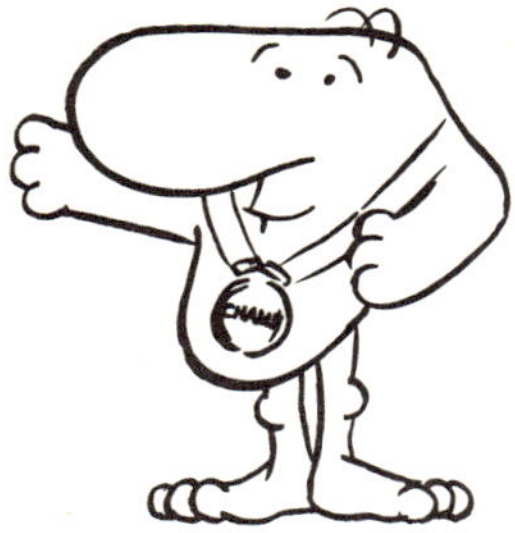

"Jesus answered [to the devil], It is written. . ." Matthew 4:4 (NIV)

Day 24 – BE A WINNER WITH THE WORD!

To be victorious over temptation, you must **follow** the example of Jesus Christ! He refuted each temptation from Satan with the Word of God - so must you! The Bible contains verses with which to resist every temptation that comes to you. In the chart below, look up God's response in His Word to each of Satan's temptations and then write God's answers in your own words.

Satan's Temptation	God's Response	In my own words, this means:
"Hey, if it feels good, do it"	Romans 8:5	
"Go ahead and do your own thing. You don't have to listen to God or anybody else."	Galatians 5:19-21	
"After all, everybody's doing it so it can't be that bad."	II Timothy 4:3,4	
"Go on - just this one time won't hurt."	James 1:15	
"Look, God is going to forgive you afterwards anyway."	Galatians 6:7,8	
"Nobody will be able to find out about it."	Numbers 32:23	
""Nobody's perfect - go ahead."	I John 2:1	

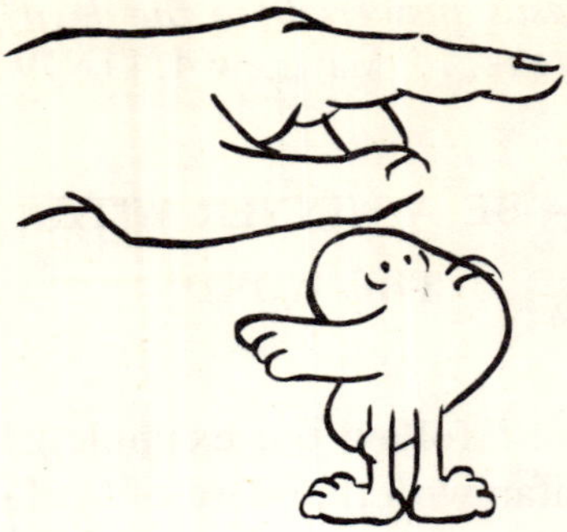

"I will instruct you and teach you in the way you should go; I will counsel you and watch over you." Psalm 32:8 (NIV)

Day 25 – GOD'S GUIDANCE AND DIRECTION

So many Christians have been caught up in trying to discover God's will and direction for their lives that they have missed the thrust of what the Bible teaches. The Bible stresses that believers should strive for holiness and purity. "It is God's will that you should be holy . . ." (I Thessalonians 4:3)

The main emphasis for all Christians is to be obedient and concentrate on becoming more like Jesus Christ every day. God's guidance is not an **end** to be pursued; it is a **by-product** to men and women who obey Christ. In Matthew 6:33 you are told to seek God's ______________________________ and ____________________________ first in your life and He will take care of _______ your needs. However, there is a difference between your needs and your wants. God has not promised to give you all you **want** - just what you **need.**

Certainly, there are decisions and choices in your life that must be made; choices concerning friends, a future mate, what school you should attend, a career, etc. Christ's concern for your future is even greater than yours. He is not going to play "Hide and Seek" with His will for your life. You must be open and willing to obey Him and surrender your will to His plan and purposes for you. In Psalm 23:3 you have the promise that God will lead you into paths of _________________. What does this mean to you? ____

____

As you continue to walk daily with Jesus Christ, studying and applying His Word and communicating with Him in prayer, He has promised you that He will show you the direction you need to take in all of your decisions.

As you seek God's will for your life, He promises in Psalm 32:8 to do what four things? ________________________ ________________________

________________________ ________________________

(continued on next page)

List two specific areas in which you are seeking to know God's direction in your life. Begin praying today for them and record when they are answered.

________________________ Date Answered __________

________________________ Date Answered __________

"THE WILL OF GOD IS NOT LIKE A MAGIC PACKAGE LET DOWN FROM HEAVEN BY A STRING . . . THE WILL OF GOD IS FAR MORE LIKE A SCROLL THAT UNWINDS EVERY DAY . . . THE WILL OF GOD IS SOMETHING TO BE DISCERNED AND LIVED OUT EVERY DAY OF OUR LIVES. IT IS NOT SOMETHING TO BE GRASPED AS A PACKAGE ONCE FOR ALL. OUR CALL, THEREFORE, IS BASICALLY NOT TO FOLLOW A PLAN OR A BLUEPRINT, OR TO GO TO A PLACE OR TAKE UP A WORK, BUT RATHER TO FOLLOW THE LORD JESUS CHRIST."

PAUL LITTLE*

FOR FURTHER READING:

* PAUL LITTLE *Affirming the Will of God.*
INTER-VARSITY PRESS

"Trust in the Lord with all your heart and lean not on your own understanding; in all ways acknowledge Him, and He will make your paths straight."
Proverbs 3:5,6 (NIV)

Day 26 – HOW TO FIND GOD'S WILL

From the verse above, identify the three conditions you must meet to experience God's direction and guidance in your life.

(1) You must ______________________________

(2) You must not ______________________________

(3) You must ______________________________

Trusting in God is believing by faith that God will lead you in the best way. If you do not really trust God "with all your heart," can you expect Him to direct your life? In your own words, what does it mean to trust Jesus "with all your heart?" ______________________________

____

You must not lean upon your OWN understanding. This verse does **not** mean that you should not think; God expects you to use the mind He has given you. However, He expects you to make decisions from HIS point of view based upon Biblical principles, not upon **your** selfish and prideful desires. Share one experience where you did what God's Word told you to do rather than what you felt like doing. (i.e. "I took out the garbage when I was asked rather than hassling my mom about it. See Philippians 2:14)

____

____

In James 1:5, God says if you lack ____________, pray and ask Him for direction. He promises to give you insight and understanding. This wisdom will come from the Holy Spirit impressing thoughts upon your mind as you read the Bible. It will also come through the advice of Godly, Spirit-filled Christians.

The best source of guidance is the Bible. God reveals most of His will through the Bible. The more familiar you become with the Word of God, the more you will understand what He would have you to do. You don't need to ask for direction when His will is clearly stated in the Bible concerning that decision. (continued on next page)

God will never lead you to do something that is expressly forbidden in the Bible. The Bible is the final authority. It is the measuring rod for all of your decisions and choices. As you seek out God's will in the Bible, and continue to pray, trust Him to open and close doors and work through circumstances and people. He has promised guidance as you put Christ first in your life, as you daily trust in Him. (See Matthew 6:33).

Identify one specific area in which you desire to know God's will

(i.e. "Should I attend college next fall?"): ______________________________

____. To the best of your knowledge, list the advantages and disadvantages of making that decision in a particular direction.

ADVANTAGES	DISADVANTAGES
______________________	______________________
______________________	______________________
______________________	______________________

This list will not only help you to actually see in black and white the positive side as well as the drawbacks, but will also help you to pray more intelligently for God's wisdom. Also seek advice from parents, Christian friends, and church leaders. Be patient. Be prayerful. Be watchful and expectant. God in His perfect timing will reveal His answer to you.

"NINE-TENTHS OF THE DIFFICULTIES IN FINDING THE LORD'S WILL ARE OVERCOME WHEN OUR HEARTS ARE READY TO DO HIS WILL, WHATEVER IT MAY BE."

FOR FURTHER READING:

Affirming the Will of God
by Paul Little, Inter-Varsity Press

Knowing God's Will and Doing It!
by J. Grant Howard, Jr., Zondervan

"Dear friends, do not be surprised at the painful trial you are suffering, as though something strange were happening to you. But rejoice that you participate in the sufferings of Christ, so that you may be overjoyed when His glory is revealed."
I Peter 4:12,13 (NIV)

Day 27 – SO YOU NEED SUPERNATURAL STRENGTH?

Even though you may be a believer in the Lord Jesus Christ, you will not automatically be protected from difficulties and hardships. In fact, because Christians are not to go along with many of the ways and attitudes of the world, you may experience MORE problems and frustrations in your life.

The Apostle Paul describes the Christian life as a battle. You are engaged in a struggle - God is on your side, and the devil is the enemy. Satan wants you to be selfish, proud, and to conform to the standards of this world. Daily you must choose who you will follow - the Savior or Satan, self, and sin.

According to I Peter 4:12,13, the Bible tells you not to be ____________ when you face __________________ in your Christian life. Instead you are to __________________ when trials come into your life because they will help build your faith. (See also James 1:2,3)

Christians are not immune from disappointments, hurts, weaknesses, loneliness, depression, or worry. Unlike the unbeliever, as a Christian you are to **face** these troubles because God promises and assures you that He will give you the power to get through them.

God promises in Isaiah 40:29 that He will supply the ________________ you will need to withstand the pressures of life if you will turn to Him and rely on His capability. The verse also states that even though you may be ______________ and ______________, in the strength of His might you will have victory. By depending upon His resources to fight life's battles, you will overcome; on your own power, you will fail.

"Dear Lord,
Teach me to rely on YOUR strength You have promised to me, rather than my own efforts."

Right now, memorize Philippians 4:13 - "I can do everything through Him who gives me strength."

Repeat it often and think on it throughout today.

"So do not fear, for I am with you; do not be dismayed, for I am your God. I will strengthen you and help you; I will uphold you with my righteous right hand."
Isaiah 41:10 (NIV)

Day 28 – PLUGGING INTO GOD'S POWER

Problems and difficulties certainly will come your way. However, you DO have the promise and assurance of God's strength to help you through these tough times. How do you receive this power? Does God just "zap" you and suddenly you become the "bionic believer?" How do you obtain and utilize the power and might of the Lord?

The first thing you must do is to realize God's **PRESENCE.** No matter how difficult or hopeless the situation, sensing that the Lord is right there with you and recognizing the fact of His presence is where to start. List the two assurances God gives in Hebrews 13:5b:

1)______________________________ 2) ______________________________

Secondly, you must know God's **PROMISES.** Again, this will only come by your consistent daily time spent with Jesus reading the Bible. Knowing God's promises, you must believe them and act upon that belief in faith. For instance, God promises in Philippians 4:19 that He will supply

____. BELIEVE AND CLAIM THAT PROMISE. YOU DON'T HAVE TO WORRY - GOD IS IN CONTROL!

Thirdly, **PRAY** to Him and ask Him for His strength and power. Look up James 4:2. One of the reasons you do not have is because you do not

____________. The Lord will give you His power; but, you must trust God to supply you with the strength He has promised.

Lastly, you **PRAISE** God and thank Him for His control in the situation and the promise of His strength. Why does the Psalmist thank and

praise God in Psalm 118:28? ______________________________________
As you recognize and praise God for Who He is through an act of faith, you then need to leave the problem with Him, knowing the Lord will help you through it.

By realizing God's **PRESENCE**, believing His **PROMISE**, asking through **PRAYER**, and thanking in **PRAISE**, you will experience God's strength and power in your life.

The verse for today, Isaiah 41:10, tells you that you should never ________________. List the five promises God gives you in this verse:

1. ____

2. ____

3. ____

4. ____

5. ____

Write down a specific problem you are struggling with in your life: ________ ____. Now practice the 4 "P" Method to realize God's power and peace in your life. The only way you'll realize God's power is if you will personalize this project.

"What a Friend we have in Jesus
All our sins and griefs to bear.
What a privilege to carry
Everything to God in prayer.
O what peace we often forfeit
O what needless pain we bear.
All because we do not carry
Everything to God in prayer."

APPENDIX A

OTHER RELATED SCRIPTURES

DAY 1 – Jeremiah 31:3, John 3, I John 4:7-21

DAY 2 – Romans 5:1, Ephesians 2:8, 9; Hebrews 11

DAY 4 – Colossians 2:6-15

DAY 5 – Psalm 103:17, Lamentations 3:22, Deuteronomy 7:9, John 4:2, I Peter 5:7

DAY 7 – Romans 1:17, 3:28, 5:1; II Corinthians 5:7

DAY 8 – Romans 10

DAY 9 – Psalm 12:6, 119:89, 119:105; John 5:39, II Timothy 3:16, I Peter 1:24, 25; James 1:21

DAY 10 – Matthew 7:13-23

DAY 12 – Psalm 40:4, Isaiah 30:15, Hebrews 10:22, 11:6; Proverbs 16:20

DAY 15 – Matthew 6:12, Acts 2:38, 10:43; Romans 3:24, 25

DAY 18 – Psalm 101:7, Proverbs 12:22, Romans 12:17, 13:13; II Corinthians 8:21

DAY 20 – Mark 14:38, Luke 22:40, Ephesians 6:13, James 1:12-14, II Peter 3:17

DAY 22 – Proverbs 1:10, 6:27; Hebrews 2:18, Matthew 4:1-11

DAY 25 – Deuteronomy 31:8, Psalm 23:2, 3, 37:23, 48:14, 106:9, 107:7, 139:9, 10, 24; Isaiah 49:10, 58:11; John 10:3

DAY 26 – Psalm 22:4, 5; Psalm 71:1, Proverbs 2:1-11

DAY 28 – Daniel 3:17; Psalm 121:2, 145:11; Matthew 19:26, Isaiah 40:28-31

APPENDIX B

God loves You and desires to give to you Peace, Joy, and Eternity in Heaven

WHAT YOU NEED TO KNOW:

1) God loves you and has a wonderful gift for you.

   John 3:16 *"For God so loved the world that He gave His one and only Son, that whoever believes in Him shall not perish but have eternal life."*

   Romans 6:23 *"For the wages of sin is death, but the gift of God is eternal life in Christ Jesus our Lord."*

2) You cannot obtain this gift of eternal life on your own.

   Titus 3:5 *"He saved us, not because of righteous things we had done, but because of His mercy."*

   Ephesians 2:8, 9 *"For it is by grace you have been saved, through faith - and this not from yourselves, it is the gift of God – not by works, so that no one can boast."*

3) You need to come into a right relationship with God in order to receive this gift of eternal life.

   John 3:3 *"I tell you the truth, unless a man is born again, he cannot see the Kingdom of God."*

   John 5:24 *"I tell you the truth, whoever hears My word and believes Him who sent Me has eternal life and will not be condemned."*

4) God sent Jesus Christ to be your way to experience forgiveness of sins and eternal life.

   II Corinthians 5:21 *"God made Him who had no sin to be sin for us, so that in Him we might become the righteousness of God."*

   I Timothy 2:4, 5 *"For there is one God and one mediator between God and men, the man Christ Jesus, who gave Himself as a ransom for all men."*

   I Peter 3:18 *"For Christ died for sins once for all, the righteous for the unrighteous, to bring you to God."*

5) God's time for you to receive this gift is NOW.

   II Corinthians 6:2 *"I tell you,* **now** *is the time of God's favor, now is the day of salvation."*

   Proverbs 27:1 *"Do not boast about tomorrow, for you do not know what a day may bring forth."*

WHAT YOU NEED TO DO:

1) Admit you have a need. ("I am a sinner.")

   Romans 3:12 *". . . there is no one who does good, not even one."*

   Romans 3:23 *"for all have sinned and fall short of the glory of God."*

   James 2:10 *"For whoever keeps the whole law and yet stumbles at just one point is guilty of breaking all of it."*

2) Acknowledge that Jesus Christ died for you on the cross of Calvary, rose from the dead, and is today with God the Father in Heaven. ("I believe Jesus Christ is the Son of God, and He alone can provide salvation for me.")

   Acts 4:12 *"Salvation is found in no one else, for there is no other name under heaven given to men by which we must be saved."*

   Romans 10:9, 10 *"That if you confess with your mouth, Jesus is Lord and believe in your heart that God raised Him from the dead, you will be saved. For it is with your heart that you believe and are justified, and it is with your mouth that you confess and are saved."*

3) Affirm your belief in Jesus by now inviting Him to come in and forgive you of your sins and control every area of your life. (I receive Jesus Christ as my Saviour and Lord.)

Revelation 3:20 *"Here I am! I stand at the door and knock. If anyone hears my voice and opens the door, I will go in and eat with him, and he with me."*

John 1:12 *"Yet to all who received Him, to those who believed in His name, He gave the right to become children of God."*

WHAT YOU NEED TO PRAY:

"Dear God,

I admit that I am a sinner. Please forgive me of all of my sins and help me to be what you want me to be from this moment on.

Jesus, I now invite you to come into my life. Thank you for dying on the cross for me so I could have eternal life. I now put my complete trust in you alone for eternal life.

Thank you for coming into my heart and saving me now. *In Jesus' Name, Amen."*

WHAT YOU NEED TO REMEMBER:

If you prayed this prayer, you have just begun a meaningful and new life with Jesus Christ.

To experience God's **Best** in your Christian life, you need to:

B – Begin Bible reading and application each day to help you to know Jesus better.

E – Every day talk to God your Father in prayer. Be open and honest!

S – Share your faith in Christ with others. Start right now!

T – Take time to attend a Bible preaching and believing church where you can learn more about how to grow as a Christian and fellowship with other Christians.

If appropriate, please fill out and send the response form to us so we can rejoice with you and pray for you.

☐ I prayed the prayer in this booklet, accepting Jesus Christ. I know this means He forgave me and came into my life.

☐ I want to rededicate my life to Christ and let Him express His love through me.

DATE

NAME — AGE

ADDRESS — PHONE

CITY — STATE — ZIP CODE

DETACH form on dotted line, complete and mail today in an envelope to:

Discipleship, Inc.
5105 Fairfield Avenue
Fort Wayne, Indiana 46807

APPENDIX C

MY PRAYER LIST

My Requests To God	Date Asked	Date Answered

Spiritual Bodybuilders

These insights from God's Word are for you to memorize and apply to your everyday living for spiritual strength. Each promise was carefully selected to assure you of God's faithfulness in each area of your new life in Christ.

Cut the verses out and carry them with you. Memorize the verses and go over them during spare minutes throughout the day. Use them daily, review them daily, and you're ready to grow!

ASSURANCE OF GOD'S LOVE

I have loved you with an everlasting love.

(NIV) Jeremiah 31:3a

ASSURANCE OF GOD'S ANSWERING PRAYER

If you remain in me and my words remain in you, ask whatever you wish, and it will be given you.

(NIV) John 15:7

ASSURANCE OF GOD'S SALVATION

I write these things to you who believe in the name of the Son of God so that you may know that you have eternal life.

(NIV) I John 5:13

ASSURANCE OF GOD'S GUIDANCE

Trust in the Lord with all your heart and lean not on your own understanding; in all your ways acknowledge him, and he will make your paths straight.

(NIV) Proverbs 3:5,6

ASSURANCE OF GOD'S FORGIVENESS

If we confess our sins, he is faithful and just and will forgive us our sins and purify us from all unrighteousness.

(NIV) I John 1:9

ASSURANCE OF GOD'S POWER

I can do everything through him who gives me strength.

(NIV) Philippians 4:13

ASSURANCE OF GOD'S HELP IN TEMPTATION

No temptation has seized you except what is common to man. And God is faithful; he will not let you be tempted beyond what you can bear. But when you are tempted, he will also provide a way out so that you can stand up under it.

(NIV) I Corinthians 10:13

ASSURANCE OF GOD'S PRESENCE

Never will I leave you; never will I forsake you.

(NIV) Hebrews 13:5b

Tips For Memorizing

Begin with one verse and read it over a number of times to understand and grasp its meaning.

Divide the verse up into natural phrases and memorize the first phrase. Then go on to the second phrase and so on.

Memorize the reference to each verse as well and review these verses each day as you carry them with you.

ASSURANCE OF GOD'S ANSWERING PRAYER

If ye abide in me and my words abide in you, ye shall ask what ye will, and it shall be done unto you.

(KJV) John 15:7

ASSURANCE OF GOD'S LOVE

Yea, I have loved thee with an everlasting love.

(KJV) Jeremiah 31:3a

ASSURANCE OF GOD'S GUIDANCE

Trust in the Lord with all thine heart; and lean not unto thine own understanding. In all thy ways acknowledge him, and he shall direct thy paths.

(KJV) Proverbs 3:5,6

ASSURANCE OF GOD'S SALVATION

These things have I written unto you that believe on the name of the Son of God; that ye may know that ye have eternal life, and that ye may believe on the name of the Son of God.

(KJV) I John 5:13

ASSURANCE OF GOD'S POWER

I can do all things through Christ which strengtheneth me.

(KJV) Philippians 4:13

ASSURANCE OF GOD'S FORGIVENESS

If we confess our sins, he is faithful and just to forgive us our sins, and to cleanse us from all unrighteousness.

(KJV) I John 1:9

ASSURANCE OF GOD'S PRESENCE

I will never leave thee, nor forsake thee.

(KJV) Hebrews 13:5b

ASSURANCE OF GOD'S HELP IN TEMPTATION

There hath no temptation taken you but such is common to man: but God is faithful, who will not suffer you to be tempted above that ye are able; but will with the temptation also make a way of escape, that ye may be able to bear it.

(KJV) I Corinthians 10:13

PERSONAL NOTES